Unbelievable Fun Facts and Trivia: 1,000 Fun Facts

Steven Bristol & Michel Clarks

1,000 Fun Facts

According to nutritional values, the daily requirement of vitamin B6 can be provided by 2.9 pounds Nutella.

* * *

A man on average gets eleven erections per day. Nine during his sleep.

* * *

The Australian prisoner Joseph Bolitho Johns broke out of prison so often that the police built a special prison cell for him. He also broke out of this.

* * *

A study from 2002 showed that 60 percent of people cannot have a ten minute conversation without having lied at least once.

* * *

Nutella was invented during World War II, when an Italian soldier mixed chocolate with hazelnut to stretch his food ration.

* * *

In Japan, people believe that one's blood type affects one's personality. For this reason, the Japanese version of Facebook has a drop-down menu for one's blood type.

* * *

The reflex that we automatically lead a small wound to our mouth is an innate protective mechanism. The saliva in our mouth helps the blood to coagulate and kills bacteria.

* * *

In 2011, scientists flew 100 paper planes from a height of 23 miles above Germany. Some of these paper planes have been found in Canada, USA, Australia and South America.

* * *

Araucana chickens are also referred to as Easter egg chickens, because their eggs can be blue, green, red or brown.

* * *

During the day, clouds fly higher than during the night.

* * *

At the age of 17, young Pattie Mellette got pregnant and was forced to have an abortion by her parents. She refused. Her child is Justin Bieber.

* * *

Family Guy is prohibited in the following countries: Indonesia, Iran, Vietnam, Taiwan, Egypt, South Africa, South Korea and Malaysia.

* * *

The colder your bedroom is, the higher is the likelihood of having a nightmare.

* * *

Because of the large amount of sugar in it, it is impossible for honey to spoil. Even in 1,000 years it would still be edible.

* * *

The increased use of the drug Sumatriptan can lead to a green coloration of the blood.

* * *

Bart Gets an F - the first episode of the second season of The Simpsons, is the most viewed Simpsons episode.

* * *

Because intelligent people think faster, their handwriting is sloppier.

* * *

In preparation of the movie Rocky Sylvester Stallone asked the former professional boxer Earnie Shavers to beat him multiple times in the face at full force. Stallone vomited after his first punch.

* * *

As early as 1966 Ford released the first electric car, which had a range of more than 200 miles. A sodium-sulphur accumulator was used as a battery. After an accident in rainy weather, the hot sodium leaking from the battery mixed with water and ignited. There was a fire that was difficult to extinguish. As a result, the model was reset and sodium-sulphur batteries were no longer used in vehicles.

* * *

By his 13th birthday, Mike Tyson had already been arrested 38 times.

* * *

For car races, Nissan only uses the number 23 on their vehicles, since in Japanese number two is pronounced as ni and three as san. Together this gives ni-san.

* * *

The glass globe above the German Reichstag building symbolizes that politics should always be transparent and that the people stands over the government.

* * *

The most common fracture in the human body is the collarbone.

* * *

Everything you write into your Facebook status, is irreversibly sent to Facebook - regardless if you actually post it.

* * *

There was already McLobster, McSpaghetti and McPizza, on offer at McDonald's.

* * *

The Towers of the World Trade Centre had their own zip code: 10048 New York.

* * *

The X-Men No. 1 is the best-selling comic book in the world with a total of eight million copies sold.

* * *

The place with the lowest gravitational pull is in Canada.

* * *

Wildlife goldfishes can live up to 40 years.

* * *

The first flags of pirates were red, not black.

* * *

Rock Bottom Remainders is a music band in which Simpsons creator Matt Groening and book author Stephen King are members.

* * *

Babies are born with 300 bones. In adulthood this number decreases to 206.

* * *

An average cloud weighs about 1.5 million pounds.

* * *

Australia exports camels to Saudi Arabia.

* * *

When McDonald's opened a restaurant in Rome in 1986, demonstrators handed out free pasta to counter McDonald's fast food.

* * *

Carde is the roman god for door handles, door sills and door hinges.

* * *

An iPad with apps installed weighs more than an iPad without apps installed.

* * *

The likelihood of getting bitten by a human in New York is higher than the likelihood of getting bitten by a shark in the sea.

* * *

The inventor of cotton candy was also a practicing dentist.

* * *

Cats are the most popular pet in the United States. There are 88 million cats compared to 74 million dogs.

* * *

From 200 decibels, music can be fatal, because then the air
vesicles in your lung can burst.

* * *

In 1999 the founders of Google wanted to sell their company
to one of its biggest competitors Excite for one million dollars
but were rejected.

* * *

The word gym comes from Greek and translates to place of
the naked.

* * *

Grapes explode when you heat them in a microwave.

* * *

Muhammad Ali is the only famous person whose star on the
Walk of Fame is not on the sidewalk itself but on the wall of a
building. He did not want people trampling on his name.

* * *

On June 30th, 2015, there was a leap second. One second was
added to the last minute of this day.

* * *

The Batman series from the 1960s was known for its
educational themes. The viewers were invited to fasten their
seatbelts in the car, do homework, drink milk and eat
healthily.

* * *

Eight out of ten people who have been struck by lightning are male.

* * *

In almost all of his songs, Lenny Kravitz does not only sing, but also plays all instruments in a recording studio.

* * *

An average U.S. citizen consumes as many resources as 32 people in Kenya use during the day.

* * *

Nintendo means temple of heavenly responsibility.

* * *

The Zoological Garden in Berlin is the largest zoo in the world.

* * *

Since 2010, Google has bought on average one company a week.

* * *

In 1952 Albert Einstein received the offer to become President of Israel. He refused.

* * *

Adolf Hitler was nominated for the Nobel Peace Prize in 1939.

* * *

Kenneth Bainbridge, scientific director of the Manhattan Project, commented at the first test of a nuclear bomb with Now we are all sons of bitches.

* * *

In the movie Halloween the villain Michael Myers wears a mask. In order to save production costs, they bought a Captain Kirk mask and simply painted it over.

* * *

The book Everything men know about woman consists of 100 blank pages.

* * *

Fingernails grow approximately four times faster than toenails.

* * *

James Harrison is a record holder in blood donations. He donated his blood over 1,000 times.

* * *

The role of John McClane in Die Hard actually went to Arnold Schwarzenegger - however he declined the role.

* * *

The 2022 World Soccer Championship will be opened in Lusail (Qatar), a city which did not exist till recently.

* * *

More than 800 castles are currently on sale in France.

* * *

Eggs can explode in the microwave.

* * *

If you bathe in alcohol, you can get drunk.

* * *

There are more people with obesity than malnutrition worldwide.

* * *

Vagina is the Latin word for sheath.

* * *

In 1913, Adolf Hitler, Joseph Stalin, Leo Trotsky, and Sigmund Freud all lived close to each other in the immediate vicinity of Vienna, and regularly went to the same cafe without ever having come into contact with each other.

* * *

If you could fold a piece of paper 42 times, that piece of paper would be able to reach the Moon.
* * *

In the state prison of Indiana, the occupants may keep cats.

* * *

Taiwan was the first country to provide free Wi-Fi to all citizens.

* * *

Twelve newborn babies are given to false parents every day.

* * *

John Adams, the second president of the United States once said I have come to the conclusion that one useless man is called a disgrace; that two are called a law firm; and that three or more become a Congress!

* * *

In Japan, it is socially acceptable to sleep while working. It is perceived a sign of hard work.

* * *

The Golden Gate Bridge is made up of so many wire ropes that put together they would circle the earth three times.

* * *

Students get better test results when looking at a green landscape during the test.

* * *

The human is the only mammal which cannot swallow and breathe at the same time. We lose this ability when we start talking.

* * *

The average rent for a one room apartment in Manhattan is 3,400 dollars.

* * *

Sound spreads through steel about 15 times faster than through air.

* * *

The children of the nephews of Adolf Hitler had voluntarily sterilized themselves, in order for the Hitler bloodline to become extinct.

* * *

The election slogan Yes we can actually comes from Bob the Builder.

* * *

To keep up with speedsters, the police of Dubai are equipped with Ferraris and Lamborghinis.

* * *

When your fingers swell from being underwater too long, it is because of an evolutionary trait of your nervous system. The fingers swell so as to provide more grip in wet conditions.

* * *

The Italian San Marino is the oldest republic in the world.

* * *

The most popular quotes from Barney Stinson from How I Met Your Mother are Have you met Ted?, Wait for it, What up and Suit up and are already mentioned in the first episode of How I Met Your Mother.

* * *

Monowi in Nebraska has only one inhabitant and he is also
mayor of the city.

* * *

Each year, about one million new employees are hired by
McDonald's in the U.S.

* * *

David Hasselhoff secured the rights to his nickname The Hoff
and the phrase Do not Hassel the Hoff as part of his divorce
settlement.

* * *

Nearly 65 percent of all autistic people are left-handed.

* * *

The Scottish kilt originally came from France.

* * *

The gravity on the moon is about one-sixth of the earth's
gravitational pull.

* * *

In France there is a village named Pussy.

* * *

The Jewish boxer Salamo Arouch was imprisoned in a
concentration camp during World War II and was forced to
fight against other inmates. The loser was shot or gassed.

* * *

There area road systems where music is played when a car
drives at the right speed.

* * *

The holes in Swiss cheese are called eyes. A Swiss cheese
without eyes is called blind.

* * *

If you Google elgooG, you will get to a mirrored Google.

* * *

The founder of Victoria's Secret sold the company for a
million dollars in 1982 and committed suicide in 1993 by
jumping off the Golden Gate Bridge.

* * *

Neptune, Saturn and Venus are the names of three seaside
resorts in Romania.

* * *

Four out of five people sing in the car.

* * *

In 2008, a Brazilian tied 1,000 balloons to a chair and flew
into the air. Two weeks later his corpse was found in the sea.

* * *

2013 became the first year after 1987 not to contain a
repeating digit.

* * *

If you twist both index fingers very slowly in a clockwise
motion and then move them faster, the circles suddenly move
in the opposite direction.

* * *

To find out whether a female is capable of mating, male
giraffes beat their heads on the female's belly until they
urinate. The male can determine the female's fertility by the
smell of her urine.

* * *

More than 250,000 millionaires live in New York.

* * *

Shakuntala Devi holds the world record in mental arithmetic.
In 1980 a computer randomly chose the two 13-digit numbers
7,686,369,774,870 and 2,465,099,745,779, which Devi had to
multiply. It took her only 28 seconds for the correct answer:
18,947,668,117,995,426,462,773,730!

* * *

In 1893, a U.S. citizen made an application to change the
name of the country to The United States of the Earth.

* * *

When the game Twister was released in 1966, it was described
as sex in a box.

* * *

On January 1 1985, the first phone call was made using a
cellular phone.

* * *

GTA originally was meant to be a racing game named Race'n'Chace but a glitch made police cars ram into the car of the player. This element was so popular with the game testers that a whole game was modelled on this principle and GTA was born.

* * *

Because people born blind smile from birth, scientists have concluded that smiling is a genetically determined behavior which is not learned.

* * *

If you salt a pineapple, it tastes sweeter.

* * *

Gary Numan is older than Gary Oldman.

* * *

Approximately 96 percent of all French secondary schools have condom vending machines on their grounds.

* * *

The largest cat in the world had a length of 1.36 yards.

* * *

On average, a person farts 14 times a day.

* * *

Google uses camels with a camera attached in the desert to get images for Google Street View.

* * *

In Stockholm, Sweden, there is speed camera which raffles the
income from speeding tickets among those who drive at the
correct speed.

* * *

Koala bears, monkeys and humans are the only animals with
an individual fingerprint.

* * *

From a statistical point of view, women are the better drivers,
as they cause less accidents.

* * *

There are so many languages in the world that it is not known
how many there currently are. Scientists believe that there are
more than 6,500 to 7,000 different languages.

* * *

In ancient Babylon it was tradition for every woman to go to
the Temple of Aphrodite at least once in her life to have sex
with a stranger.

* * *

The oldest ever found advertisement dates back to 3,000 BC
and was found in the ruins of Thebes. It advertised a slave
named Shem.

* * *

Nearly one in five Germans regularly use a laptop on the
toilet.

* * *

In terms of the level of medical accuracy, Scrubs is the best medical television series in the world.

* * *

If you feel very connected to a person, you can hear their voice in your head when you read messages they have sent.

* * *

Every year, about 4 million cats are consumed as delicacies in China.

* * *

The human is the only primate who has no bone in his penis.

* * *

The DNA among humans differs by just 0.1 percent. In comparison, a chimpanzee is genetically different from humans by 1.2 percent.

* * *

In an online petition, 87,000 people voted for McDonald's to serve a vegetarian burger.

* * *

O. J. Simpson was freed, among other things, because it was proved that the investigator was biased. In a telephone conversation, he mentioned the word Nigger more than 40 times.

* * *

Left-handers on average live longer than right-handers.

* * *

90 percent of people start fake laughing when they do not
understand what others have said.

* * *

The heart of a shrimp is located in its head.

* * *

It takes eight minutes and 17 seconds until the light from the
sun reaches the earth.

* * *

In 1981 a hard disk containing one gigabyte cost 300,000
dollars.

* * *

When crying tears of joy, the first one mainly comes from the
right eye, while the first tear of sorrow mostly comes from the
left.

* * *

When rebels stormed the home of Muammar al-Gaddafi, they
discovered a photo album with pictures of the former U.S.
Secretary of State Condoleezza Rice.

* * *

Due to more accurate methods in GPS surveying, the official
size of Liechtenstein in Europe was corrected by 10,760
square feet in 2014.

* * *

Every 21st inhabitant of New York is a millionaire.

* * *

Adult cats exclusively meow to communicate with humans.

* * *

The combination of a knife with a fork and a spoon is called spork.

* * *

The average income of an intern at Facebook and Snapchat is between 8,000 to 10,000 dollars a month.

* * *

About 89 percent of all men have problems with differentiating between kind behavior from a woman and flirting.

* * *

Since the end of the Second World War, Japan has apologized in official statements more than 50 times for its acts during the war.

* * *

Bangladesh, although just one percent the size of Russia, is more populated.

* * *

Sneezing too intensively can cause a broken rib.

* * *

The word alphabet consists of the words alpha and beta, which are the first two letters in the Greek alphabet.

* * *

Studies have proved that an increase in the amount of homework correlates with the increased likelihood of students to become depressed.

* * *

In order to make wolf puppies urinate, their mother has to lick their bellies with her warm tongue.

* * *

Corals are chemically so similar to human bones that they are used to treat fractures.

* * *

$-40\ °F = -40\ °C$

* * *

The most common cause of death in Germany for men and women is coronary heart disease.

* * *

Although women's brains are slightly smaller, they are more efficient then men's brains.

* * *

Astronauts in the ISS can witness 15 sunrises and 15 sunsets a day.

* * *

Before she became famous, the singer Pink worked for
McDonald's.

* * *

At birth, the blue-whale baby is already 23 feet long and
weighs more than two tons.

* * *

If you enter Beam me up, Scotty as a search term on
YouTube, all videos are beamed to the screen.

* * *

The two most common reasons for a bad temper are hunger
and insufficient sleep.

* * *

Each year about 100 million bikes are produced worldwide.

* * *

When the Cornhuskers - the football team of the University of
Nebraska- have a home match, the stadium becomes the third
biggest city in the state.

* * *

In the Trevi Fountain in Rome 3,000 Euros is thrown in by
tourists every day.

* * *

From 1781 to 1850, the planet Uranus was named George.

* * *

There is more bacteria on your own skin then there are living people in the world.

* * *

Humans are the only species that cook their food.

* * *

The real name of actor Michael Keaton is Michael Douglas.

* * *

In 1987 American Airlines was able to save 40,000 dollars because they used one less olive in their salads.

* * *

The clitoris has more than 8,000 nerve endings, while the penis just has 4,000.

* * *

The vagina has a self-cleaning mechanism.

* * *

Translated into Spanish Colgate means hang yourself.

* * *

The national animal of Scotland is a unicorn.

* * *

Humans and dolphins are the only animals, which have sex solely for pleasure.

* * *

Since 1964, in memory of the victims of the atomic bomb, the flame of peace is burning in Hiroshima, which will only be extinguished once all nuclear weapons on the earth have been eliminated.

* * *

The 100 richest people in the world earned so much money last year that they could end global poverty four times over.

* * *

According to his driving license, Spongebob was born on July 14, 1986.

* * *

One side effect of aspirin is headache.

* * *

In the special edition 3 of the Club Nintendo comic book series, the reader finds out that Kirby smokes, drinks and eats unhealthy fast food.

* * *

Only two percent of all people have green eyes.

* * *

Frank Oz, the voice of Yoda in Star Wars, was also the voice of Miss Piggy.

* * *

Women who frequently play video games have more sex than other women.

* * *

A bite of the Brazilian wandering spider can cause men an erection that lasts for hours.

* * *

Only five percent of all humans have red hair.

* * *

In 1994 a man was arrested in Los Angeles for scaring elderly people. He dressed himself as the grim reaper and looked inside the windows of the elderly.

* * *

If you start counting from one, then 1,000 is the first number in which the letter A occurs.

* * *

A fifth of all people use their smartphone during sex.

* * *

The city with the longest name in the world is Llanfairpwllgwyngyllgogerychwyrndrobwllllantysiliogogogoch and is located in Wales.

* * *

The more educated a couple is, the lower the probability of divorce.

* * *

The maiden name of Goethe's mother was Textor.

* * *

One of the founders of the DNA structure - James Watson - was forced to sell his Nobel Prize in 2014 due to financial problems. He received 4.1 million dollars and the buyer gave him the Nobel Prize back afterwards.

* * *

Star Trek was the first TV series to show a kiss between a white man and a black woman on TV.

* * *

Water only gets the typical chlorine smell when someone pees in the basin.

* * *

In 1879 the Belgian mail service launched a pilot project in which cats were used to deliver the letters. The project failed.

* * *

Scorpions can survive for up to one year without food.

* * *

In Turkmenistan, water, gas and electricity has been free to citizens since 1991.

* * *

The spider species Caeristris darwinispins the largest webs in the world. Their size can reach more than ten feet.

* * *

Four percent of all people do not fold their toilet paper, but scrunch it together instead.

* * *

Most people are born in August.

* * *

A study came to the conclusion that female students, who are perceived as attractive by their fellow male students, achieve better grades.

* * *

A pineapple was such a large status symbol in 18th century England that you could rent it for a day.

* * *

Sperm contains only five calories. So it only gets you fat when you are pregnant.

* * *

In Iceland, Greenland and the Antarctic there are no ants.

* * *

450 men die of breast cancer in the U.S. each year.
* * *

A human could survive two minutes in space without a space suit.

* * *

It is assumed that cats are responsible for the extinction of several animal species.

* * *

There is a woman whose name is actually Marijuana Pepsi Jackson.

* * *

On average, German women have their first baby at the age of 29.

* * *

The highest ever documented weight of a human being was 1,400 pounds.

* * *

A U.S. court had to decide if the X-men are humans or not. In the US, imported dolls representing human beings are subject to a higher tax than other toys. As of this a toy manufacturer sued for a declaration that the action figures did not represent human beings to pay lower taxes.

* * *

The designer Ko Yang has invented a milk package that changes its color when the milk begins to spoil.

* * *

In Lazio (Italy) policemen drive Lamborghinis.

* * *

About 60 million people who are alive today, will die within the next 12 months.

* * *

The word blood is mentioned at least once in every
Shakespeare piece.

* * *

Worms can have up to ten hearts.

* * *

George Washington was known to spend approximately seven
percent of his annual salary on alcohol.

* * *

Thanks to collaboration with Twitter, every public tweet sent
in the U.S., is digitally archived in the Library of Congress.

* * *

The first president of Zimbabwe was President Canaan
Banana.

* * *

The oldest bar in Ireland, which still exists, was opened 900
years before Christ.

* * *

After watching the series Breaking Bad, Hannibal actor
Anthony Hopkins wrote a letter to Bryan Cranston, the main
character of the series, and told him: Your performance as
Walter White was the best acting I have seen - ever.

* * *

Ransom payments to abductors can be written off as taxes in
Germany.

* * *

In Iowa, a 99 year old senior woman sews one dress every day
to donate them to children in Africa.

* * *

Butterflies are cannibals.

* * *

In 1970, roughly six billion dollars was spent on fast food.
Nowadays, it is about 200 billion dollars.

* * *

In the U.S. state of Minnesota, a three-year-old was mayor for
a short time.

* * *

Bodies transported by an airplane are denoted by HUGO for
Human Gone.

* * *

It is unknown where Mozart was buried.

* * *

The human eye reacts so well to light that it could see the
flame of a candle in absolute darkness from about 30 miles
away.

* * *

Instead of LOL people in France say MDR for mort de rire, which means laughing to death.

* * *

When the ninth symphony came out, Beethoven had already become deaf and could not hear it anymore.

* * *

Bushes and clouds in Super Mario Bros have the same shape, only the color is different.

* * *

In medieval France, women were among others punished by being forced to catch a chicken in the city while naked.

* * *

In the 18th century the Briton Mary Toft became famous for giving birth to rabbits. Years later she was sentenced to death when it became clear that she just put dead rabbits in her vagina, which she pushed out later on.

* * *

When it comes to extreme heat in Melbourne, the lions in the zoo are given frozen blood.

* * *

Based on an interview, Pope Francis watched television for the last time on the 15 July 1990.

* * *

In its language selection, Facebook offers the language pirate.

* * *

The Sims was originally designed as an architecture simulator.

* * *

Alcohol protects against radiation.

* * *

One study documents that many people, after two years of
obtaining their tertiary qualifications, remember only ten
percent of the content they have learned.

* * *

In Norway, you pay half the amount of normal tax in
December, to have more money for Christmas.
* * *

If. There. Is. A. Period. After. Every. Word. Our. Brain.
Automatically. Starts. Making. Pauses. After. Each. Word.

* * *

In the 17th century, New York was called New Amsterdam.

* * *

The intelligence of a child is primarily determined by its
mother.

* * *

The longest beard ever measured on a woman had a length of
10 inches.

* * *

Because a big butt is a sign of fertility, men feel more attracted to women with larger butts.

* * *

Nomophobia describes the fear of not being available via mobile phone.

* * *

A newborn just has 234 milliliters of blood in its body.

* * *

Edgar Bergen was the first man to win an Oscar made of wood for his ventriloquial performance.

* * *

The human circadian rhythm is better suited to life on Mars than on Earth.

* * *

Paparazzi is Italian and can be translated to annoying mosquitoes.

* * *

From a water depth of 33 feet and more it becomes impossible to fart.

* * *

During the Second World War a special event was held in a
news magazine. Two soldiers were betting who would be the
first to kill 100 enemy soldiers with a sword. Both died before
they could win the competition.

* * *

In third world countries, residents can access Wikipedia via
their smartphone without using their data. The Wikipedia Zero
campaign is already available in 34 countries.

* * *

A person has between 100,000 and 150,000 hairs on their
head.

* * *

Jonah Falcon has the biggest penis in the world. It has a length
of almost 14 inches.

* * *

Leonardo DiCaprio was named after Leonardo da Vinci. His
mother was looking at a drawing by the artist in a museum,
when she felt young Leonardo move for the first time.

* * *

The Sagrada Familia in Barcelona has been under construction
for over 130 years and is still not finished.

* * *

In 1976 the BBC made an April fools hoax, that the planets in
our sun system are located in a special constellation so that the
gravity is decreased. This resulted in more than one thousand
calls, confirming that one actually can feel the effect.

* * *

On average, a raindrop reaches a speed of 21.7 miles per hour.

* * *

If you could drive directly to the moon by car at a speed of 80 miles per hour, it would take about four months to reach it.

* * *

In 2014, Red Bull spent a billion dollars on marketing, but only 600 million dollars on the production of beverages.

* * *

Scientists assume that the face of the Sphinx was painted red.

* * *

The capital of Kazakhstan is Astana. Which when translated means capital.

* * *

Tom Hanks brother - Jim Hanks - sounds very much alike his brother, which is why he occasionally does synchronization work for him.

* * *

Walt Disney has received 63 Oscar nominations throughout his lifetime, of which he has won 26. Thus, he is the world record holder of most Oscar wins.

* * *

Arnold Schwarzenegger was meant to play the role of Kyle Reese in the movie Terminator.

* * *

Ryan Gosling was short-listed to be in the Backstreet Boys.

* * *

Male kangaroos flex their biceps to impress females.

* * *

In 1967, a former Prime Minister of Australia disappeared without a trace and has still not been found.

* * *

From water depth of 33 feet and more there is no more red light. For this reason blood seems to be green at this depth.

* * *

Dubai uses falcons to keep their cities free of pigeons.

* * *

In 1923, a dead rider finished first in a horse race in New York. The rider suffered a heart attack during the race and the horse carried the dead body to the finishing line.

* * *

The inventor of the Game Boy was initially a janitor at Nintendo.

* * *

The Big Ben has its own Twitter account with 450,000 followers. Every hour a new tweet with Bong, Bong, Bong appears, whereby the number of bongs varies with the hour.

* * *

To date, 43 Germans have won an Oscar and 81 have been awarded the Nobel Prize.

* * *

Gray whales exclusively mate in a threesome.

* * *

About 31 percent of Germany's surface is covered by forest.

* * *

Flipper was played by five different dolphins.

* * *

Goats have rectangular pupils.

* * *

Rabbits have such good peripheral sight they are able to see things behind their head.

* * *

Renfield-Syndrome is characterized by an obsession with drinking blood.

* * *

Chinatown in New York is the largest settlement of Chinese citizens outside Asia.

* * *

The drug lord Pablo Escobar had so much cash in his home that rats ate about a billion dollars of his wealth per year.

* * *

In Stockholm Sweden, there is a pilot project, which involves receiving an SMS when someone has a heart attack nearby and the ambulance has been called. Then the receiver can rush to the location and execute a heart lung massage. So far 9,500 people have joined this project and in 54 percent of the cases, people reach the location before the ambulance and are able to provide assistance.

* * *

Falling asleep next to a loved one helps one to doze off faster and decreases the risk of depression.

* * *

Currently, there are about seven billion people on earth who make experiences and memories every day. A total of 220 years of new human memories are generated per second.

* * *

Hulk originally was meant to be a grey monster but as the printing works had problems to always use the identical shade of grey, the creators decided to turn Hulk green.

* * *

Since 1896, soccer fields in Germany have to be free of trees.

* * *

Chris Putnam is a developer at Facebook and has immortalized himself in social networks. If one writes :putnam: in a comment, one will see his face as a smiley.

* * *

In 2013, more people died in the United States from children playing with small guns than from terrorists

* * *

In New Zealand, there is a lake, which on average has a temperature of 147 degrees Fahrenheit due to geothermal processes.

* * *

The Foreign Accent Syndrome describes a disease in which the affected persons involuntarily speak their mother tongue with a foreign accent.

* * *

In 2009, a ten year old tried to sell his grandma on eBay.

* * *

In Ukraine there is a 1,000 feet deep salt mine, which is used in the treatment of respiratory diseases. Due to the high salt content, there are fewer bacteria in the air than compared to the most sterile rooms of a hospital.

* * *

The record for most passengers on an airplane was set in 1991 with 1,081 people. Two babies were born during the flight.

* * *

When we talk to somebody we like, our voice changes.

* * *

Vikings took cats on sea trips in order to avoid a rat problem. Nowadays, it is assumed that this prevailed the worldwide spread of cats.

* * *

The Pineapple Incident is the most watched episode of How I Met Your Mother.

* * *

The word Tsundoku is Japanese and describes people who buy many books but never read them.

* * *

The human heart beats more than 100,000 times a day.

* * *

In Germany, almost each second marriage ends in divorce.

* * *

In terms of the number of museums, theatres and libraries, Germany is the country with the most opportunities for cultural activities.

* * *

When the first telephones came people answered there call with ahoy.

* * *

French was the national language of Great Britain for more than 300 years.

* * *

In 2005, Mark Zuckerberg offered Facebook for 75 million dollars to MySpace. The CEO of MySpace, Chris DeWolfe - declined.

* * *

The average price of one liter of black ink is higher than the price of one liter of human blood.

* * *

Playing video games increases creativity, concentration and makes you happier.

* * *

In ancient Greece the sandals of prostitutes bared an inscription, so that the words follow me appeared on the sandy ground.

* * *

British woman Wendy Southgate is most commonly seen on Google Street View.

* * *

According to Bill Gates, just a small amount of poor countries will exist in 2035.

* * *

The IKEA catalogue is the only book on earth, of which there are more copies than the Bible.

* * *

A statistician at Stanford University has already won the lottery four times and has received over 20 million dollars.

* * *

Neither Hollywood nor Bollywood produced the most movies per year. It is Nollywood in Nigeria, where about 2,000 movies are finished a year.

* * *

In the 90s, 50 percent of all CDs produced were the free AOL Internet CD.

* * *

An average vagina is three to four inches deep and can increase by up to 200 percent when the woman is aroused.

* * *

NASA claims it will be able to answer the question if we are alone in universe in the next 20 years.

* * *

To avoid baggage fees, a man from China wore 70 items of clothing on his body.

* * *

Like humans, ducks have different accents.

* * *

The blue whale is the loudest animal on earth. Its cries can be heard from a distance of 373 miles.

* * *

Statistically, most cars are stolen on New Year's Day.

* * *

In 1856 a man from Havana took off in his hot air balloon and was never seen again.

* * *

If you enter = rand () in Microsoft Word, you get a random text.

* * *

In China, the websites of BBC News, Amnesty International and the Dalai Lama are banned for the citizens.

* * *

If a man would never shave his face, his beard would be approximately 30 feet long on the day he dies.

* * *

Germany was the first country to implement summer time.

* * *

Gandhi was nominated five times for the Nobel Peace Prize, but never received it.

* * *

Russian man, Valery Spiridonov is alleged to be the first human to receive a head transplant. His head will be grafted onto another body.

* * *

When the space probes Rosetta and Philae left the earth on
March 2, 2004, there were no iPhones, Facebook existed for
27 days and nobody knew of Twitter.

* * *

The development of chemical drugs can be traced back to the
Nazis. For example, scientists in the Third Reich discovered
an active substance that helped soldiers to march 55 miles
without stopping.

* * *

The first seven seconds are the most important when making a
first impression.

* * *

Only eight percent of the world's money is physical. The rest
exists digitally.

* * *

New York is located more southern than Rome.

* * *

In Paris there is only one stop sign.

* * *

From 1789 to 1790, New York was the capital of the USA.

* * *

There are no reported incidents of death by dehydration in the
history of world running. But there are plenty of cases of
people dying of drinking to much water.

* * *

Human blood contains about 0.2 milligrams of gold.

* * *

About 90 percent of all lung cancer cases are caused by
smoking.

* * *

The people who voiced Mickey Mouse and Minnie Mouse in
the 1930s were married in real life.

* * *

There are the same amount of chickens and humans on Earth.

* * *

One gram of DNA contains as much information as could be
stored on 600 billion traditional CDs.

* * *

It is genetically determined whether you can role your tongue
or not.

* * *

A nap improves your memory and protects against heart
disease.

* * *

The table tennis ball in Forrest Gump was inserted by special
effect designers, so that Tom Hanks never had to play table
tennis.

* * *

The continent with the highest average education level is Antarctica.

* * *

Foxes use the Earth's magnetic field to estimate distances.

* * *

The Audi brand name e-tron means pile of shit in French.

* * *

The average distance a man walks on foot during his life is four times around the world.

* * *

Slugs are able to sleep three consecutive years.

* * *

In the USA, a slave from 1850 by today's standards, would cost 1,000 dollars.

* * *

In the Turkish village Halfeti, completely black roses grow each summer.

* * *

About 75 percent of all people are scared of speaking publically in front of people.

* * *

Similar to the fingerprint, each human has an individual tongue print.

* * *

If one took all the world's water and placed it into a cube, it would accommodate 39,375 cubic feet.

* * *

A moment is a medieval time unit, exactly 90 seconds. An hour therefore has 40 moments.

* * *

The molecule Penguinone got its name because of its chemical structure which resembles a penguin.

* * *

Sean Connery was wearing a hairpiece for all his James Bond movies because he already began balding at the age of 21.

* * *

The International Space Station is the most expensive object ever made by humans. It has cost 160 billion dollars so far.

* * *

Angela Merkel's middle name is Dorothea.

* * *

In France people were killed by the guillotine up until 1977.

* * *

In 2009, Marc Aurus - an expert on the prevention of kidnapping - gave a lecture on the topic of How to avoid being kidnapped in Mexico and was then kidnapped.

* * *

Since 2013, every citizen of Uruguay is allowed to buy 40 grams of marijuana at a pharmacy for their own personal use. Due to the good price of one dollar per gram, as specified by the state, many former drug lords have left the now unprofitable drug business.

* * *

In Italy, a man left his cat an inheritance of about ten million Euros.

* * *

Jim Cummings, the voice of Winnie Pooh in the U.S., regularly calls seriously ill children in hospitals and talks to them in his Winnie Pooh voice to delight them.

* * *

The highest temperature ever measured in a human body was 115.7 degrees Fahrenheit.

* * *

In 2012, the CEO of Lenovo received an annual bonus of three million dollars. Instead of keeping the money for himself, he distributed it among his 10,000 employees.

* * *

Cats cannot taste sugar.

* * *

The average depth of the oceans is 2.5 miles.

* * *

The more you burp, the less you have to fart.

* * *

Sharks were on the earth before trees existed.

* * *

Scientists have demonstrated that cats have the same brain patterns as humans have during sleep. It is therefore assumed that cats can dream.

* * *

Sony has developed a refrigerator which exclusively is opened while smiling.

* * *

Penguins can jump six feet high.

* * *

On the distant planet HD 189733b it rains molten glass at wind speeds of 4,350 miles per hour.

* * *

In the U.S., a man stole several million dollars after having beaten a security system consisting of security guards, infrared sensors, motion detectors and a safe door. He was arrested when DNA traces were discovered on the remainders of a sandwich that was found in a trash can next to the crime scene.

* * *

The S in the name of Harry S. Truman only represents an S.

* * *

Regular sex can relieve nasal congestion and help treat asthma
and hay fever.

* * *

Ten percent of all car accidents are caused by being distracted,
for example when writing an SMS.

* * *

The original name of the movie Scream was Scary movie.

* * *

Annually, more people die from being hit by a champagne
cork than from the bite of a venomous spider.

* * *

The deaf cannot get seasick.

* * *

Hugh Hefner has become almost completely deaf in recent
years. Doctors believe his increased use of Viagra is the cause.
Hefner however, says that he would rather be deaf than forgo
sex.

* * *

The movie French Kiss is called English Kiss in France.

* * *

Big Ben is only the name of the main bell in the belfry of London. The correct name of the bell tower is Clock Tower.

* * *

The 1996 Nokia Communicator was the first ever smartphone, it cost 800 dollars and even had a fax connection.

* * *

The superhero Flash is faster than Superman.

* * *

The actor Robin Williams was passionate about video games, which is the reason why he named his daughter Zelda.

* * *

Django Unchained was the first movie in sixteen years in which Leonardo DiCaprio wasn't the highest paid actor on set.

* * *

In the 1940s, the Coca Cola Company developed a colorless version of Coca Cola specifically for the USSR.

* * *

The vaginal fluid of women can be found in sharks.
* * *

The term Checkmate comes from the Persian phrase Shah Mat which means the king is dead

* * *

The Wall of China cannot be seen from space - however,
China's smog can.

* * *

One pound of muscles burns 16,300 calories per year.

* * *

The shoe size of the Statue of Liberty is size 879.

* * *

By law, cars are prohibited on Mackinac Island in Michigan
since 1898. Inhabitants use horses instead.

* * *

In the Middle Ages green was the colour of love.

* * *

According to Amazon, the best-selling books on Kindle are
the Bible, the Steve Jobs biography and the Hunger Games
trilogy.

* * *

According to estimates, the iPhone is the most profitable
product in the world. About 50 percent of the selling price is
Apple's profit.

* * *

The construction of the Titanic cost seven million dollars. The
film starring Leonardo DiCaprio cost 200 million dollars to
produce.

* * *

Scientists of Stanford University observed that a walk can increase people's creativity by up to 60 percent.

* * *

A Jamais-vu is the opposite of a Déjà-vu.

* * *

Central Park in New York is larger than the State Monaco.

* * *

It is estimated that 7,000 people die every year because the handwriting of the treating doctor was not legible.

* * *

Martin Goodman - one of the founders of Marvel - thought Spider-Man was a bad idea because people do not like spiders.

* * *

During a press conference in the 70's a reporter asked Stevie Wonder, what it was like being born blind. He answered It could have been worse. I could have been born black.

* * *

It only takes one drop of engine oil to contaminate more than 25 liters of water.

* * *

Polar bears are left-handed.

* * *

The first server at Google was built from legos.

* * *

In France it is prohibited by law, to name a pig Napoleon.

* * *

The deepest gold mine in the world is located in South Africa, and is situated 2.5 miles below the surface.

* * *

The first person shooter Half Life has already been successfully used in the treatment of arachnophobia (the fear of spiders).

* * *

It is a long tradition in Ireland to leave a bottle of beer at the front door for Santa Claus.

* * *

Pornhub once started campaign called Save the Boobs. For every 30th view in the category small tit or big tit, the company donated one penny to the Susan G Komen Foundation - a foundation whose aim is to cure breast cancer. However, the foundation refused the donation. Therefore, Pornhub tripled the amount of money and donated it to a foundation with a similar purpose.

* * *

All of our school textbooks show the solar system with the planets close enough to fit on one page. In actuality if you were to draw the solar system to scale and the earth was the size of a pea on paper Jupiter would be over 300 meters away and Pluto would be 2 and a half kilometers away. The nearest star would be 16,000 kilometers away on paper.

* * *

Only a few special types of piranhas eat meat. All others feed on plants.

* * *

In Cambridge (Canada) you can pay your parking ticket by donating soft toys.

* * *

During the Olympic Games in China, Usain Bolt ate only chicken nuggets, as it was the only meal he recognized from home. Ultimately, he won three gold medals with this diet.

* * *

The indents on a golf ball are called dimples.

* * *

Researchers in Australia are working on a new condom made of cellulose that is 30% thinner but 20 percent more robust.

* * *

About 80 percent of people breathe exclusively through one nostril. Which nostril is used by the body varies approximately every 2.5 hours. While the other nostril is not being used for breathing, the body cleans it.

* * *

Before McDonald's offered burgers, the company sold hot dogs.

* * *

Men more frequently dream of other men, while women dream of both sexes equally.

* * *

The majority of Canada's population lives south of Seattle.

* * *

A phenomenon referred to as the CSI effect explains when jurymen become influenced by television series such as CSI Miami.

* * *

Sleeping on your belly can lead to crazier, creepier and more sexual dreams.

* * *

The police of Saudi Arabia have a special witches-unit, where people can report cases of magic. Fortune telling is also considered a crime.

* * *

In 1647 Christmas was forbidden by the English Parliament.

* * *

To prove their credibility in court in early Rome, men have sworn on their balls.

* * *

Nepal is the only country in the world that does not have a rectangular flag.

* * *

Goosebumps are a reflex from the times when man had much more hair. When our hair stands up, we appeared bigger and more menacing to enemies.

* * *

An adult oyster can clean and filter up to 190 liters of water per day.

* * *

The song Hey ya by Outkast says Shake it like a Polaroid picture, forced Polaroid to release a press release that shaking a Polaroid too much can damage the picture.

* * *

Tibetan monks sleep while sitting.

* * *

In South Africa there is a bar in a 6,000 year old tree.

* * *

There is actually a website about Barney Stinson's fake character Lorenzo von Matterhorn from How I Met Your Mother: www.lorenzovonmatterhorn.com.

* * *

Blind people are able to dream and to see pictures in their dreams.

* * *

On average, a man ejaculates 7,200 times during his entire life.

* * *

Because of the reduced distance to the central core of the earth at the equator, people at the equator weigh less than people at the poles.

* * *

The thermometer was invented in Italy.

* * *

If you listen to The Proclaimer's song I'm Gonna be (500 miles) while on board on the international space station, you will have travelled approximately 1,000 miles or 500 miles and 500 more.

* * *

McDonald's is the biggest customer of Coca Cola.

* * *

The actor Mark Wahlberg was suspended from school after just a few years and therefore never finished it. To be a shining example to his kids, he catched up in his high school diploma in the age of 42.

* * *

Einstein believed that mankind would only survive four years after the extinction of bees.

* * *

The most common words in the world are ok and cola.

* * *

The entire human population could live in New Zealand, and the population density would still be lower than that of Manhattan in New York.

* * *

Some survivors of Hiroshima showed an unusual reaction. Due to the high radiation dose they were subjected to, their finger nails became black and bled slightly.

* * *

Although the Incas had a huge empire, they did not possess money. The inhabitants paid their taxes in the form of man power and got food in exchange for this.

* * *

When the Mona Lisa was stolen from the Louvre in 1911, Pablo Picasso was one of the suspects.

* * *

Redheads are less sensitive to pain and more sensitive to temperature when compared to people with different hair colors.

* * *

In Texas, there is a city called Earth; it is the only place in the
world named Earth.

* * *

Koala bears hug trees to cool down on hot days.

* * *

If the earth were as large as a sand grain, the sun would be as
large as an orange.

* * *

People cry the amount it would take to fill one bath tub in their
whole life.

* * *

For fun, a British couple invited the Queen to their wedding.
The Queen actually came to the wedding.

* * *

One bite of the Inland-Taipans - the most poisonous snake in
the world - injects enough poison into its victim to kill more
than 230 people.

* * *

Stephen Hawking has now surpassed the life expectancy
estimated by doctors by 50 years.

* * *

The Amazon is home to pink dolphins.

* * *

In Cambodia you can buy pizzas with marijuana as a topping.
It is called Happy Pizza.

* * *

Washing your hands regularly with soap and water is a
sufficiently protective mechanism against the Ebola virus.

* * *

At Starbucks laughing is part of the job description.

* * *

During the production of Toy Story 2, an employee
accidentally erased the whole movie and almost ruined the
production. Fortunately, one of the employees had a backup
on her desktop computer, so the work went on and the movie
made it to the cinemas.

* * *

With total assets of 1.5 billion dollars, Snapchat founder Evan
Spiegel is the world's youngest billionaire.

* * *

According to NASA, Jurassic Park is the seventh best movie
in the world, measured in terms of scientific accuracy.

* * *

Liliy's high school lover, Scooter from How I Met Your
Mother , is the husband of Barney actor - Neil Patrick Harris -
in real life.

* * *

In the movie Pulp Fiction all clocks show the same time: 4.20
o'clock.

* * *

Approximately 70 percent of the world's total oxygen is
released by plants in the oceans.

* * *

Parkinson's Law describes the fact that an employee needs as
much time for a task as he has available for it.

* * *

Listening to music is the only activity which involves all areas
of the brain.

* * *

City birds are now integrating cigarette stubs into their nests
as they have recognized that these are effective against insects.

* * *

In Mumbai you can take out insurance against dodging paying
of fares.

* * *

In 2014 a woman was saved from her burning house. She then
realized she had forgot her mobile phone in the house, ran
back into her home and died.

* * *

When two wolves mate, they stay together for the rest of their
lives.

* * *

In space you cannot burp.

* * *

The westernmost point of the USA and the easternmost point of Russia lie just three miles apart.

* * *

An American married the Eiffel Tower in 2007.

* * *

The longest distance at which a sniper has killed his target is 2,707 yards. The bullet flew through the air for a total of six seconds.

* * *

Pac-Man was originally named Puck Man

* * *

There is a Barbie doll which is modelled after Angela Merkel.

* * *

Jonas Salk refused to take out a patent on his polio vaccine. He commented that: There is no patent. Could you patent the sun?

* * *

There is no physical description of Jesus in the Bible.

* * *

In Australia, the cheapest wine is cheaper than the cheapest bottle of water.

* * *

Instead of using lawn mowers, Google has about 200 goats that graze the grass on the Google site.

* * *

When being asked for his IQ, Stephen Hawking answered: I have no idea. People who boast about their IQ are losers

* * *

About 99,99999999999% of an atom is nothing. If one would eliminate the empty space of all atoms from the entire human race, the remaining mass would fit in a coffee mug.

* * *

More than 50 percent of the world's population has never received a phone call.

* * *

The penis foreskin of burn patients can be used for healthy skin growth.

* * *

Barney Stinson from How I met your Mother is the real inventor of the Bro-Code. Based on Google search analytics the term hadn't existed before 2008.

* * *

In Alaska there is a sand desert with dunes up to 160 feet high.

* * *

Gladiators in ancient Rome were exclusively fighters who fought against other humans for life and death. People fighting exclusively against animals were called Bestiarii.

* * *

The word mafia refers to the criminal organization in Sicily. Comparable structures in other regions use their own names like Camorra or Yakuza.

* * *

Scientist support that on Enceladus, a moon of Saturn, streams of water can be found.

* * *

It took one year to sell a million copies of the first iPhone. With the iPhone 6, a million copies were sold on the first weekend of its release.

* * *

Octopi have three hearts.

* * *

Mothers instinctively kiss their newborn baby. Through the kiss the mother takes up bacteria and viruses of the child and forms antibodies which can pass through the mother's milk to the child.

* * *

Based on a fan petition, LEGO launched the production of a special Big Bang theory set in 2015.

* * *

Facebook is blue because the founder Mark Zuckerberg
suffers from red-green color blindness.

* * *

The first call with a mobile phone was made by its inventor,
Martin Cooper. He called a rival to brag about his
achievement.

* * *

A study concluded that people with a lower IQ more
frequently tend to be more homophobic and racist than people
with a higher IQ.

* * *

Laughing one hundred times burns the same calories as a 15-
minute workout on the bike.

* * *

In 539 BC the Persian king Cyrus the Great adopted the first
human rights of the world. He thus freed all slaves and gave
people the right to decide for themselves what they wanted to
do.

* * *

Hippopotami on average kill 2,900 humans per year, stags
130, ants 30, cows 22, horses 20 and sharks only five. But
who would run away from a cow?

* * *

On the basis of number of viewers, Disney's Jungle Book was
the most successful movie in Germany.

* * *

The abbreviation X-Mas for Christmas can be traced back to
the ancient Greeks. The X stands for the Greek letter Chi
which used to be the abbreviation for the word Christ.

* * *

In 1930 Ketchup was sold as medicine.

* * *

Contraceptive pills also work for gorillas.

* * *

Nowadays, 82 percent of young people do not ring doors
anymore, but send a message that they have arrived and wait
outside the door.

* * *

About 99 percent of all Estonians have blue eyes.

* * *

A study has shown that four percent of all people dream
exclusively in black-and-white.

* * *

E.T. was originally a horror movie, in which aliens reach the
earth and kill humans by touching their heads with their
fingers.

* * *

Human gastric acid is so corrosive that it could dissolve a
razor blade.

* * *

In Amsterdam there is a gym where you can train naked.

* * *

According to current estimates, it would cost more than 23 billion dollars to build a real Jurassic Park.

* * *

In summer the Eiffel Tower is 5.9 inches higher than in winter.

* * *

To prepare for her tour, Beyoncé always sings while jogging.

* * *

Because all passports in UK are officially issued by the Queen, she does not own a passport. When travelling abroad she just has to state that she is the Queen.

* * *

Pizza is one of the few words that is understood almost everywhere in the world.

* * *

Strawberries are not berries, but in fact nuts.

* * *

So far about 270 people have had their bodies frozen, to be revived in the future.

* * *

On average a spacesuit costs eleven million dollars.

* * *

Young elephants like to suck on their trunks just like young children like to suck on their thumbs.

* * *

After Josef Stalin had heard that his son failed to commit suicide, he said: He can't even shoot straight.

* * *

The Swedish man Max Martin is the most successful music composer in the world. Among others he wrote the songs Wish You Were Here, Quit Playing Games With My Heart, I Want You Back, Oops! … I Did It Again, It's My Life, Since U Been Gone, I Kissed a Girl, Hot n Cold, Dynamite, DJ Got Us Falling' in Love and Fucking Perfect.

* * *

When a Fiat employee realized when the Google Street View car will record Södertälje in Sweden, he parked a Fiat in front of the Swedish Volkswagen headquarter to be present in Google Street View for the next years.

* * *

The deepest hole ever explored by man was 7.5 miles deep. Compared to that, the earth has a diameter of 7,926 miles.

* * *

If you write 3:) on Facebook you will see a little surprise.

* * *

After Tupac's death, his best friends mixed his ashes with
marijuana and smoked it.

* * *

May I have a large container of coffee. If you count the
number of letters of every word in this sentence you get a
good approximation for pi.

* * *

Bruce Lee was a gifted dancer. He won the Cha-Cha
Championship in Hong Kong in 1958.

* * *

Skateboard professional Tony Hawk has an IQ of 144.

* * *

Scientists believe that it is possible to exterminate all
mosquitoes, without impacting on our global ecosystem.

* * *

The least people are born in February.

* * *

The chimpanzee Congo was able to draw abstract works of art.
Even Pablo Picasso was a fan of his pictures.

* * *

The release of the film The Princess and the Frog led to more
than 50 cases in the US where children were infected with a
disease because they had kissed a frog.

* * *

In 2008 the Briton James Feley started to sell cans with nothing - i.e. an empty gift box - as a gift idea via Amazon. By now he has earned more than three million pounds by selling nothing.

* * *

After Steve Jobs' secretary was late due to her car breaking down, he later that afternoon gave her the keys to a new Jaguar, and told her, Here, don't be late anymore.

* * *

If you visit Rainymood.com you can hear the sounds of rain.

* * *

Living in the White House is not free for the President of the United States. He receives a monthly bill for food and other expenses.

* * *

During his time in school Isaac Newton wrote an essay on how water moves from the roots to the leaves in a tree. This phenomenon could first be scientifically proven about 225 years later.

* * *

When the first railroads started to operate, doctors warned of health effects, such as in the brain. This was due to its high speeds of up to 19 miles per hour.

* * *

Hans Zimmer has composed the soundtracks for Lion King, Gladiator, Pirates of the Caribbean, Inception and for the Dark Night trilogy. According to him he spent two weeks in a music class during his childhood and learned the rest by himself.

* * *

With a speed of 91 gigabits per second, NASA has the fastest internet-connection in the world.

* * *

With total assets of approximately 500 billion dollars, Black Panther is the richest superhero in the world, much richer than Batman (about 80 billion dollars) and Iron Man (about 100 billion dollars).

* * *

In Minneapolis, Minnesota, a room has been developed, for research purposes, that absorbs all sounds. If you are inside, it is so quiet that you can even hear your own pulse. However, if you stay too long in absolute silence, hallucinations may occur.

* * *

As the earth rotates more slowly around the sun from year to year, 2016 was one second longer than 2015.

* * *

Okinawa Island in Japan is the safest place in the world. More than 450 people, who are more than 100 years old, live there.

* * *

After a 19 year old girl became the three millionth follower of
Venezuelan President Hugo Chávez on Facebook, the
president gave her a house.

* * *

In the early 50s a Blow Job described the bang when breaking
the sound barrier.

* * *

In the United States at least one person per hour gets killed in
a car accident due to drinking.

* * *

The actor Morgan Freeman has already been nominated for
more prizes than he has made films.

* * *

If you shrank the earth to the size of a billiard ball it would be
just as smooth as one. You wouldn't be able to feel the
difference between Mt. Everest and the Mariana Trench.

* * *

The inner skin of a vagina is folded and opens while having
sex.

* * *

Around 75 percent of all vehicles, which were produced by
Rolls-Royce, are still in operation.

* * *

Dolphins sleep with there eyes open.

* * *

The first name of Master Yoda from Star Wars is Minch.

* * *

By licking a postage stamp, you consume 0,1 calories.

* * *

Broken Heart Syndrome is the medical term for the separation of a beloved partner. The symptoms can be so strong, that the patient gets cardiac dysrhythmia, suffers from pain and is not able to breathe properly.

* * *

There's only one country between Finland and North Korea: Russia.

* * *

In 2010, General Electrics made profits of 14 billion dollars and paid not a penny in taxes.

* * *

In 2012 about 37 percent of Italians had never used the Internet.

* * *

Between 2011 and 2013, McDonald's has opened one branch a day in China.

* * *

In 2006, scientists officially declared that the egg came first, not the chicken.

* * *

Michael Jackson was negotiating to buy Marvel.

* * *

Female lions carry out 90 percent of the lion's hunting activities.

* * *

All Scandinavian countries have a cross on their flag.

* * *

If you have a ten dollar note in your pocket and do not have any debts, you are richer than 25 percent of U.S. citizens.

* * *

Sea water has an average salt content of 3.5 percent.

* * *

It takes an average employee at McDonald's about seven months to earn the amount the CEO makes in one hour.

* * *

Facebook also allows for exotic smileys. If you write (^^^) as a comment a shark appears. With <() you see a penguin and: poop: creates a small pile of poop.

* * *

Multimillionaire Forrest Fenn, hid a treasure worth two million dollars in the Rocky Mountains. In order to find it, you have to solve a number of puzzles. Until today, nobody has found the treasure.

* * *

The more intelligent one is, the more zinc and copper can be
found in one's hair.

* * *

The maximum speed of a T.Rex was slower than the average
sprinting speed of a human.

* * *

Toilet paper was invented in China in the 13th century.

* * *

A blowjob under water is called Aquabob.

* * *

Koalas sleep about 90 percent of their lives.

* * *

If you are immune against a minimum of aluminium you have
an alumuniumminimumimmunity

* * *

Golf balls were originally made of wood.

* * *

If 57 people are gathered in one room, the likelihood of two of
the people having their birthday on the same day, is about 99
percent.

* * *

Tsutomu Yamaguchi was working in Hiroshima when the first atomic bomb hit the city. As he was driving home to Nagasaki the second bomb hit. He is currently 90 years old and still alive.

* * *

The teeth of limpets are the hardest biological material in the world.

* * *

If you watch all Saw movies at once, it will take you 666 minutes.

* * *

Johnny Depp always has his Jack Sparrow costume while travelling and visits children in hospitals regularly as Captain Jack Sparrow.

* * *

A study came to the conclusion that the lack of movement in the Western world kills the same amount of people as smoking does.

* * *

In 1925, Coca-Cola published a key pendant in the shape of a swastika.

* * *

Yellow teeth are more robust than white teeth.

* * *

Brryan Jackson's father infected his son with HIV at the age of eleven months to kill him, because he didn't want to pay alimony. Within 5 years the doctors diagnosed AIDS in Jackson. They gave him just a few months. Today, Brryan Jackson is 20 years old and HIV has not been detected in his blood for more than five years.

* * *

Being in love releases the same hormones that the use of cocaine releases.

* * *

The astronomer Eugene Shoemaker is the only human whose ash was transported to the moon after his death.

* * *

Babies already dream in their mother's womb.

* * *

Celery has negative calories - it costs more energy to digest it.

* * *

Once, Charlie Chaplin took part in a Charlie Chaplin imitator contest and came in third place.

* * *

People with blue eyes have a higher tolerance threshold for alcohol and are therefore drunk only after consuming larger quantities of alcohol.

* * *

In Australia, a hog stole 18 beers from a camping site, got drunk and then tried to attack a cow.

* * *

Approximately 20 percent of the French landmass is outside of Europe. For example the islands Martinique and Guadeloupe are in the Caribbean Sea.

* * *

In 2010 a professor at the Kansas State University wanted to show his students that during a diet only the amount of calories is important, and not the nutrients. For two months he almost exclusively ate candy and lost more than 26 pounds.

* * *

To date, it is not clear why people and other animals need sleep. There are many theories, but even experts are uncertain about their accuracy.

* * *

For every episode of The Simpsons the producers needed six to nine months.

* * *

In France it is not prohibited to marry a dead person.

* * *

It is impossible to sneeze with your open eyes.

* * *

In preparation for his role as Walter White in Breaking Bad
Bryan Cranston was taught by the DEA how to make meth.

* * *

Since 1944, Iceland does not have its own army, and have not
been attacked by other countries since.

* * *

The honor code of comic book authors forbids the use of
werewolves in comics.

* * *

When leaving school, a child in the U.S. has already witnessed
40,000 people dying on TV.

* * *

Female skunks are able to influence the development of their
embryos, in order to delay birth in times of food shortages.

* * *

The Bonobo Kanzi monkey is able to make its own bonfire
and cook its food in it.

* * *

Half of the memory unit, Byte, is known as a nibble.

* * *

On average, there are 88.8 weapons per 100 U.S. citizens.

* * *

In war times significantly more boys than girls are born. This is called the Returning Soldier Syndrome.

* * *

Einstein was asked what it was like to be the smartest guy in the world, he answered I don't know, ask Nikola Tesla.

* * *

After the death of Leonardo da Vinci, King Franz I. of France hung up the Mona Lisa in his bathroom.

* * *

Eminem's mother sued the rapper because he insulted her several times in his songs. She received damages of 1,600 dollars.

* * *

In Lapland, the horns of reindeers are sprayed with reflective color so that they can be seen better in the dark and car accidents can be prevented.

* * *

Leonid Rogozovy is the only human to do an appendectomy with local anaesthesia on himself.

* * *

Cobie Smulder, the Robin actor in How I Met Your Mother, is actually Canadian.

* * *

Saddam Hussein had a Koran, written with his own blood.

* * *

In 2009 in Florida, a man who was accused of owning child porn, said his cat had downloaded the files.

* * *

The human heartbeat changes when listening to music and adapts to the sound.

* * *

The actress Mila Kunis suffers from heterochromia iridum. So she has two different eye colors.

* * *

The first hard disk for Apple II had a capacity of five megabyte.

* * *

Gnats are especially attracted by people with blood type O.

* * *

The name Google is derived from the word googol which denotes a one followed by one hundred zeros.

* * *

In Spain there is a comedy club in which you pay per laugh.

* * *

In 1983 Marvel released a comic series called Spider-Pig. The main character was Peter Porker.

* * *

From the time Pluto was discovered, about 75 years ago, it has
only traveled one-third the distance around the sun

* * *

Sweden has the least amount of murders each year.

* * *

Due to global warming, the sea level rises by approximately
three millimeters each year.

* * *

The Islamic movement Moro Islamic Liberation Front calls
itself MILF.

* * *

Due to reduced air pressure, water on Mount Everest boils at
158 degrees Fahrenheit.

* * *

The reason why actor Morgan Freeman wears earrings is due
to a maritime tradition. They wore their earrings, so that their
own burial could be paid with them, in case of their death.

* * *

In one second an average two people die.

* * *

In the USA, there is a sports league for rock-paper-scissors
competitions.

* * *

The London Underground now makes more profit by selling
its popular underground maps than it does operating the
subway.

* * *

A Scottish study found that most heart attacks happen on a
Monday.

* * *

In 1958 an atomic bomb disappeared from the arsenal of the
U.S. Army in Georgia. To this day it has not been found.

* * *

It takes the sun 226 million years to circumnavigate the Milky
Way.

* * *

Pumba from The Lion King was the first Disney character
who was allowed to fart.

* * *

Netflix has over 20 million subscribers in China even though
Netflix is not available in China.

* * *

Peanuts are not nuts but in fact beans.

* * *

The oldest high-school graduate in Germany is 73 years old.

* * *

Besides humans, ants and bees are the only animals to wage
war against members of the same species.

* * *

The term money laundering can be traced back to Al Capone,
as he used Laundromats for this purpose.

* * *

It takes about 100,000 years for the sun's energy to penetrate
out from the core of the sun to the outermost layer and only
eight minutes until it reaches the earth.

* * *

In 1938, Adolf Hitler was Time Magazine's Person of the
Year.

* * *

There is a programming language called ArnoldC, which
consists only of quotes by Arnold Schwarzenegger.

* * *

The full name of Yoshi is T. Yoshisaur Munchakoopas.

* * *

Seen chronologically, Cleopatra was closer to the moon
landing than to the construction of the pyramids.

* * *

A behavioral study came to the conclusion that brunette
women are perceived as more intelligent by their peers than
women with other hair colors.

* * *

There is a type of jellyfish which is immortal.

* * *

On Jupiter and Saturn it rains diamonds.

* * *

When cows eat too many carrots, their milk can turn pink.

* * *

Just five percent of all babies suck their left thumb. The remaining 95 percent use their right one.

* * *

A study has shown that people with a lot of body hair have on average a higher IQ than people with less body hair.

* * *

The medical term for headaches due eating to ice-cream is sphenopalatine ganglioneuralgia.

* * *

In ancient Rome the punishment for rapists was their genitals being smashed between two stones.

* * *

People in Norway who own electric cars, are allowed to park everywhere for free, do not have to pay for the ferryboat and can drive in the bus lane.

* * *

In the history of Mexico, on one occasion, there were three presidents on one day.

* * *

When the pirate Jean Lafitte learnt of a bounty on his head of 500 dollars was issued by the governor, he issued a bounty on the governor's head of 5,000 dollars.

* * *

Genetically, humans possess the requirements for hibernation.

* * *

The likelihood of dying in your cab on the way to the airport is higher than to die on your flight.

* * *

An ostrich can run a marathon in less than 60 minutes.

* * *

In terms of stress levels people aged 18-33 face the hardest challenges.

* * *

Besides Steve Jobs and Steve Wozniak there was a third founder of Apple: Roland Wayne. He sold his shares in 1976 for 800 dollars.

* * *

The Golden Gate Bridge has to be painted regularly. The salt water corrodes the paint so fast, that one has to start repainting the bridge as soon as one is finished painting it.

* * *

In eight cities in Italy, an elevated level of cocaine and marijuana in the air can be documented.

* * *

The first cloned cat has been called CC as an abbreviation for carbon copy'.

* * *

In order to avoid a long-standing dispute, the CEO's of Southwest Airline and Stevens Aviation decided to resolve their problem by arm wrestling. The winner was given the right to use a specific advertising slogan.

* * *

As opposed to one skyscraper in 1991, Dubai now has over 400.

* * *

The often mentioned Bro Code and Playbook are real books, which can be bought.

* * *

Lifetime paid 750,000 dollars per episode for the worldwide distribution rights on the TV show How I Met Your Mother.

* * *

The longest sentence in a book can be found in Les Miserable. It consists of 823 words.

* * *

In summer, storks poop on each other's feet in order to cool down.

* * *

Vin Diesel invested 3,000 dollars to produce the film Multi Facial. The film was about his problems getting a real major role. Steven Spielberg watched the movie and cast Vin Diesel for his first major role in „Private James Ryan". From then on his career began.

* * *

The former U.S. Marine soldier Guy Gabaldon was able to catch about 800 Japanese soldiers during World War Two. The Japanese soldiers were hiding in a cave and Guy Gabaldon sneaked in. He convinced them that their cave was surrounded. After everyone was handcuffed he called for support.

* * *

Family Guy is the first television series which, after being cancelled, came back to TV, because the DVD sales were so high.

* * *

Bob Marley's song No Woman No Cry was actually called No Woman Nuh Cry. This song is not about the better life of men without women, but about the life of a sad woman.

* * *

If you close your eyes and try to walk straight, you are involuntarily inclined to walk in circles. There is currently no explanation found by scientists as to why this happens.

* * *

Cats sweat through their paws.

* * *

Frederic Baur developed the boxing of Pringles Chips. After his death in 2008, his ashes were buried in a Pringles box.

* * *

In the U.S. most movies are released on Independence Day. Conversely, the movie Independence Day was released a week prior to Independence Day.

* * *

The largest hydrogen bomb that has been detonated caused such a big shock wave that it could still be measured after the third circumnavigation of the globe.

* * *

The most economically unprofitable movie in U.S. history is ZYZZXD Road. It earned a total of 20 dollars.

* * *

Mars is the only known planet which is inhabited solely by robots.

* * *

The first ATMs required six digits as a PIN. However, after a large number of users could not remember six digits, the PIN was reduced to four digits.

* * *

The first successful blood transfusion took place in 1660 and was between two dogs.

* * *

One million seconds correspond to about twelve days, but one billion seconds correspond to 32 years.

* * *

The cousins of Sailor Moon are Sailor Uranus and Sailor Neptune.

* * *

Short female car drivers have the highest likelihood of being killed by the cars airbag due to their close distance to the steering wheel.

* * *

Timothy Ray Brown is the first man to be cured from AIDS. In 2007 he received a bone marrow transplant due to his blood cancer. After the treatment, doctors could not detect HIV in his body anymore. To date, nobody knows how this was possible and whether the disease will come back. This phenomena could only be detected on two further people.

* * *

Each year a lying competition takes place in England. Participants have to tell a made up story for five minutes. To be fair, politicians and lawyers are not allowed to participate.

* * *

When Erich Honecker, a GDR politician, first visited the Federal Republic of Germany, his red carpet was 8 inches shorter than usual, because the Federal Republic did not want to show him the same respect as other citizens and friends.

* * *

Russia has more land mass than Pluto.

* * *

In biological terms, love is an addiction. The serotonin level among lovers is as low as among drug dependents.

* * *

Diabetic patients are unable to regulate their blood glucose level. For this reason, the glucose level is sometimes so high that even the urine of a diabetic patient would taste sweet.

* * *

Barney Stinson from How I Met Your Mother has worn the ducky tie in 11 episodes.

* * *

On the small island of Limone sul Garda in Italy the inhabitants have developed a genetic mutation that makes it impossible for them to have a heart attack.

* * *

When the Big Bang theory was presented for the first time scientifically, it was rejected by many scientists because it seemed too religious.

* * *

Michael Jackson proposed a Harry Potter musical, but J. K. Rowling refused.

* * *

High heels were originally worn by men to look taller. It was only in the 17th century that women began to wear such shoes in order to be more masculine. The result was that men were no longer wearing high heels, so as not to look feminine.

* * *

McDonald's earns 8.7 billion dollars a year though franchise revenue only. That is more than the gross domestic product of Mongolia.

* * *

In Australia in 2009, snipers were tasked with defending a colony of penguins against possible enemies to guarantee the survival of this rare penguin species.

* * *

It takes 40 minutes to cook an ostrich egg.

* * *

Each year around 1,000 people die because they are struck by lightning.

* * *

Babies are not able to taste salt until they are four months old.

* * *

The area on earth, which is suitable for coffee plants to grow,
is called the bean belt.

* * *

Most accidents at work happen on Mondays.

* * *

The human brain needs 33 milliseconds to determine the mood
of a person, from their facial expressions alone.

* * *

If you had invested $100 in Bitcoin in 2010, you'd be worth
more than $70 million now.

* * *

Leonardo da Vinci loved animals so much that he often
bought caged animals to set them free.

* * *

An anonymous donor pays for the college tuition of each
student in Kalamazoo, Michigan.

* * *

Our blood accounts for seven percent of our body weight.

* * *

When James Cameron was in a Roman hospital due to food
poisoning he had a nightmare about a robot from the future
trying to kill him. From this idea he created the script for
Terminator.

* * *

It is possible to die even 24 hours after drowning. People who die from dry drowning do not tend to notice their discomfort while the water continues to spread in their lungs until they die.

* * *

In the U.S., the probability of suicide is twice the rate of an assassination by a third party.

* * *

A study proved that men really have problems understanding women's feelings.

* * *

The dance style Daggering was forbidden on Jamaican television, as it lead to numerous penis fractures during the dancing.

* * *

About 83 percent of German women would abstain from sex for 100,000 Euros.

* * *

In Singapore, it is forbidden to chew gum. Only a few people are allowed to do so for medical reasons.

* * *

The speculum - a tool for gynaecologists - was already used 1,300 years before Christ.

* * *

NASA plans to grow crops on the moon in the next six years.

* * *

In the last 3,000 years, there were only 268 years in which no wars occurred.

* * *

Pablo Escobar - the world's biggest drug lord - had so much cash that he had to spend 2,500 dollars a month on rubber bands that held his money together.

* * *

Pierce Brosnan was contractually prohibited from wearing suits in other films during his time as James Bond.

* * *

To protect the German soldiers from the British night vision technology, they spread the lie that eating lots of carrots helped British soldiers to increase their eyesight during night. A myth was born.

* * *

When Hitler visited during World War Two, activists cut the elevator cables of the Eifel Tower so that he had to climb the stairs all the way to the top.

* * *

In the 1960s, a female fan hid in postal package and was sent by a friend to the Beatles' address. The postal services however, discovered and freed the lady before she was able to be posted.

* * *

Terminator 2, The Silence of the Lambs, The Beauty and the Beast and the Prince of Bel Air are closer in time to the moon landing than on today's date.

* * *

When Mario had his first act in Donkey Kong in 1981, his name was Jumpman.

* * *

If you Google 241543903 you get numerous pictures of people who have put their heads in the refrigerator.

* * *

J. K. Rowling - the author of the Harry Potter books - is no longer a billionaire. She has donated most of her fortune.

* * *

If you hold a grain of sand against the night sky, it will hide 10,000 galaxies from your eyes.

* * *

The sun is actually white. But our atmosphere makes it look yellowish to us.

* * *

The Tammar wallaby has a weight of only one gram at birth.

* * *

The Harvard physicist Lene Hau was successful in reducing the speed of light to 38 miles per hour.

* * *

Because it was impossible to transport the ingredients needed for Coca Cola in Nazi Germany, the Coca Cola Company designed a beverage especially for the German market: Fanta.

* * *

The first car accident with fatalities happened in 1896 at a speed of less than four miles per hour.

* * *

Just one percent of all heart attacks is caused by sex whereas ten percent are brought about by getting up too fast.

* * *

Before there were trees on the earth, our planet was covered by giant mushrooms.

* * *

Because emus and kangaroos are not able to walk backwards, they are officially referred to as heraldic animals of Australia.

* * *

At the beginning of the 20th century, radium was often used as an ingredient in facial cream.

* * *

Adolescents are increasingly suffering from sleep deprivation. The reason for this is, among other things, the early start of school.

* * *

Every year around 600 lightning bolts strike the Statue of Liberty.

* * *

The full name of Mr. Burns is Charles Montgomery Plantagenet Schicklgruber Burns.

* * *

Approximately 200,000 new people are born each day.

* * *

Two of the richest men in the world - Bill Gates and Warren Buffett - officially stated that they will donate 90 percent of their assets when they pass away.

* * *

In Estonia, Wi-Fi is made freely available to all citizens - even to the 90 percent who live in the forests.

* * *

Apple owns more cash than the United States.

* * *

The Hard Rock Cafe T-shirts are the world's best-selling T-shirts.

* * *

During How I Met Your Mother there have been 13 interventions. The most popular ones were Barneys frequent usage of magic tricks, Marshals addiction to charts and Lilly's fake British accent.

* * *

99

The record for The most orgasms in one hour is 134 for
women and 16 for men.

* * *

Around 35 percent of all billionaires have never graduated
from higher education.

* * *

The former U.S. politician Thomas Jefferson believed that
every law should automatically become void after 19 years, to
be replaced by a new law, which is adjusted to the new
generation.

* * *

McDonald's sells 75 burgers per minute.

* * *

To date, about 5,000 people have already turned their ashes
into an artificial diamond after death.

* * *

In the 1960s, the Barbie model Slumber Party Barbie was
released, which gave children extra tips on how to lose weight.
One of them was that you should not eat anything.

* * *

During the 19th century in the UK, the sentence for an
unsuccessful suicide attempt was death by hanging.

* * *

In 1867 the USA bought Alaska from Russia for just 7.2 million dollars.

* * *

The weirdest things that have been found in food sold by McDonald's are: bandaging material, the head of a chicken and a dead rat.

* * *

McDonald's also delivers its food - in at least 18 countries around the world.

* * *

There are more public libraries in the U.S. than McDonald's restaurants.

* * *

The U.S. channel Fox has the rights on the Simpsons until 2082.

* * *

According to a survey from 2008, about 58 percent of British teens believed that Sherlock Homes really existed.

* * *

The Lily actress Alyson Hannigan from How I Met Your Mother is married to Alexis Dennis in real life, the actor of news reader Sandy Rivers.

* * *

At the beginning of the 20th century, horses created so much dirt with their excrement, that cars were regarded as the green alternative.

* * *

Women blink more frequently than men.

* * *

Japanese people believe that black cats bring good luck.

* * *

The real Top Gun School imposes a five dollar fine to anyone in the staff that quotes the movie.

* * *

During the making of the film Star Wars - Return of the Jedi Knights a number of crew members surrounded the actor playing Chewbacca in forest scenes to guarantee his safety. They were afraid that hunters might think he was Bigfoot.

* * *

The Cookie Monster from Sesame street is actually named Sid

* * *

In Iran 70 percent of all science students are female.

* * *

Rice has more genes than humans.

* * *

The production cost of one penny is 1.7 cents.

* * *

All books in Dumbledore's library in the Harry Potter films are actually telephone books, which have been remodeled to look like old books.

* * *

The names of the main characters in the film Inception are Dom, Robert, Eames, Arthur, Mal and Saito. When you combine the initial letters of these names, you get the word Dreams.

* * *

It is assumed that so far only four percent of our oceans have been explored.

* * *

With every ejaculation a man unloads one to two teaspoons full of sperm.

* * *

After James Cameron saw Star Wars for the first time in 1977, he quit his job as a truck driver and began his career in the film industry.

* * *

All faces we see in our dreams are faces of people we have already met in real life.

* * *

Rome holds the world record for the city with most elevators.

* * *

As the water of a coconut is isotonic and sterile, it is used as saline solution in underdeveloped countries.

* * *

In Asian culture, white is a mourning colour. Therefore Asian wedding dresses are never white.

* * *

The Italian chocolate brand Italo Suisse changed its name in 2013 to Isis. One year later it had to change it again because of the rise of the terror organization.

* * *

In Switzerland there are dishwashers with cheese fondue and raclette programs.

* * *

Blind people have nightmares, and have them four times more often than normal seeing people do.

* * *

Only nine percent of consumers of marijuana are addicted.

* * *

In the 1890s Bayer, a pharmaceutical company in Germany, advertised heroine as a medicine.

* * *

To kill a spider, a woman in Kansas burned down her house.

* * *

Gottfried Svartholm, a co-founder of Pirate Bay, let his mother read instructions for using computer programs to him at the age of six, in order to learn the basics of programming.

* * *

Female kangaroos have three vaginas.

* * *

Nutella has a sun protection factor of 9.5.

* * *

People with creative professions have higher life expectancies than people with other professions.

* * *

In India there are milkshakes with marijuana.

* * *

The majority of astronauts, U.S. Presidents and Nobel Prize winners were first-borns.

* * *

Before the actor James Franco became successful, he practiced different accents while working as a cashier at McDonald's to see his customers reactions.

* * *

Pirates wore an eye patch, so they could take it off at night and so could see better in the dark.

* * *

In 2010 a pizza was sold for 10,000 Bitcoins. At today's exchange rate this would be four million dollars.

* * *

School grades are just as valuable as an indicator of intelligence as age is for personal maturity.

* * *

Frequent sex increases the growth of brain cells.

* * *

The sign Made in Germany was originally intended to warn British people of inferior items from Germany.

* * *

In 1911, the Niagara Falls froze completely.

* * *

According to a U.S. study, marriages between homosexual couples are less likely to lead to divorce when compared to marriages between heterosexual couples.

* * *

The founder of Wikipedia - Jimmy Wales - has only a fortune of about one million dollars.

* * *

Reading reduces your stress level much more than listening to music or walking.

* * *

In Dubai people own refrigerator magnets, which order a pizza by pressing them.

* * *

The world record for wearing the most underpants at the same time is at 302 pairs.

* * *

Even during the night there are rainbows. They are called moon bows.

* * *

Your mouth contains more bacteria than your anus.

* * *

A hug lasting more than 20 seconds releases so much oxytocin that we begin to trust the other person more.

* * *

The Jesus nut is the bolt that holds the rotor blades of a helicopter together. The name of the bolt was given by its importance. When it breaks, only a prayer to Jesus helps one to survive.

* * *

It would require 1,200,000 mosquitoes to exsanguinate the blood out of a human.

* * *

People who own iPhones have sex more often compared to
Android users.

* * *

In Uganda there is a kingdom called Buganda and its national
language is Luganda.

* * *

Zebras and ostriches often stay together in the wilderness.
Ostriches can see enemies at long distances, while zebras are
able to hear enemies from far away.

* * *

In Austria there are three toilets, which are listed for
preservation.

* * *

The album Hybrid Theory by Linkin Park is the most sold
debut album of the 21st century.

* * *

Because of pressure balance it is impossible to whistle in a
space suit.

* * *

Only two percent of the human population has green eyes.

* * *

The earth is the only planet in our solar system, that is not
named after a god.

* * *

When Google shut down for five minutes in 2013, the world
internet traffic decreased by 40 percent.

* * *

Only three years after the first football rules were laid down,
the hand play was forbidden.

* * *

In 2005 a used pregnancy test belonging to Britney Spears was
sold for more than 5,000 dollars on Ebay.

* * *

The Candlefish is so oily, that it used to be burned and used as
a candle.

* * *

On average, first-borns have the highest IQ among their
siblings.

* * *

The fear of long words is called
hippopotomonstrosesquipedaliophobia.

* * *

In Japan, there is an office tower in which a highway runs
though, between the fifth and the seventh floors.

* * *

When Einstein heard of the book „100 Authors Against Albert Einstein", he replied, Why 100? If I were wrong, one would be enough.

* * *

If classical music is played in wine shops, the turnover increases by 2.5 times compared to the wine shops where pop music is played.

* * *

In 1994 the iPad would have been the fastest computer on earth.

* * *

The world record for the most push-ups in one day is 46,001.

* * *

During the expansion of the railway network in Uganda, an incredible incident occurred. Two Tsavo lions repeatedly killed workers during night and slowed the construction progress. About 135 people died this way.

* * *

The explosion of a modern nuclear atomic bomb in London would produce such a large pressure wave that glass panes in Berlin would also shatter.

* * *

Panama is the only country in the world in which the sun rises above the Pacific Ocean and sets over the Atlantic Ocean.

* * *

The average person watches their favorite movie 29 times in their lifetime.

* * *

The oldest bridge in France is called Pont Neuf. Translated it means New Bridge.

* * *

Marvel originally was named Timely Comics.

* * *

The starting melody of Windows was composed on a Mac.

* * *

Schools test only your memory and not your intelligence.

* * *

Many different bacteria are located in a woman's vagina. Much of those bacteria are also found in yogurt.

* * *

Starbucks was named after the first mate of Captain Ahab in Moby Dick.

* * *

In Italy on New Year's Eve, traditionally one wears red underwear to have luck for the new year.

* * *

The Jewish population is only 0.2 percent, yet 20 percent of all Nobel prizes have been awarded to people of the Jewish faith.

* * *

Night vision devices display a green image because people can perceive the most amount of contrast in green.

* * *

An average pubic hair has a life expectancy of three weeks. A head hair lives in comparison up to seven years.

* * *

The longest 1-syllable word in the English language is strengths.

* * *

Scientists believe they have discovered an evolutionary jump. It was discovered that the Australian lizard stems from an egg-laying species to a viviparous one.

* * *

In Night of the Living Dead (1968) zombies moved at 1 step/sec. In World War Z (out today), they have sped up to 6.7 SPS.

* * *

Everyday McDonald's serves over 68 million people. This is approximately one percent of the world's population.

* * *

Because of a reduction in the emission of greenhouse gases,
scientists predict that the ozone hole will close in 2075.

* * *

The author J. K. Rowling was the first person in the world
who became a billionaire by selling books.

* * *

The founders of Adidas and Puma were brothers.

* * *

Three men from Yemen accused NASA for settling on Mars.
According to the men, their ancestors gave it to them 3,000
years ago.

* * *

Between 2009 and 2012, Alexander Bychkow killed and ate at
least nine people. According to him, he did this to impress his
ex-girlfriend, who had ended the relationship prior to the
killings.

* * *

50,000 people die a year in the U.S. from the effects of passive
smoking.

* * *

Alaska crosses the border with the eastern hemisphere and is
thus the most eastern and western state in the USA.

* * *

Your hearing is worse when you are well fed.

* * *

Swans only have one partner in their lifetime.

* * *

If all the gold in the world was melted, a dice with an edge length of 66 feet would be the result.

* * *

The WWF chose a panda for its logo, in order to save print costs and to set a sign.

* * *

The human brain consumes about 20 percent of the body's total energy.

* * *

Pandas are able to fake a pregnancy to get more food from the zookeepers.

* * *

So far, there have already been around 106 billion people in the world.

* * *

Jabbar Collins was imprisoned for 16 years. During this time he read numerous law books and found a procedural error which led to his freedom and a compensation of ten million dollars.

* * *

If you dissolve Viagra in water and give it to your plants, they remain fresh up to a week longer.

* * *

Because the movie Psycho was produced in black-and-white, chocolate syrup was used for blood.

* * *

There are just two people who know the recipe for Coca Cola. For this reason they are not allowed to be in a plane at the same time.

* * *

On a flight from Amsterdam to Boston a woman from Uganda gave birth to a child. In the end, the baby was given Canadian citizenship as it was born in their airspace.

* * *

During the nine seasons of How I Met Your Mother Ted dated 29 women who were not the mother.

* * *

Robert Lane named his two sons Winner and Loser. Winner Lane turned criminal, while Loser Lane had a successful career at the NYPD.

* * *

About 20 percent of all calories consumed worldwide comes from rice.

* * *

Scientists assume that the first human who will become 150 years old or older, has already be born.

* * *

The seven wonders of the ancient world only existed concurrently for 60 years.

* * *

YouTube Blocked in Tajikistan After a Video of the President Dancing Goes Viral.

* * *

If McDonald's was its own country, it would be the 90th biggest economy in the world.

* * *

In 1968 Kip Keino almost arrived late to the Olympic 1,500 meter run, due to a traffic jam. He therefore left the car, ran the remaining 2.5 miles to the stadium and took home the gold medal.

* * *

Microsoft sued the student Mike Rowe after he launched the site MikeRowSoft.com.

* * *

On average, people laugh ten times a day.

* * *

Coca-Cola owns the websites ahh.com, ahhh.com and so on. The website with the longest URL contains 62 hs.

* * *

In order to prevent tickets to his concerts becoming too
expensive, musician Kid Rock charges a maximum of 100,000
dollars per gig.

* * *

Since 1987 Starbucks on average opens two stores a day.

* * *

Human fingers are so sensitive that they can feel objects of 13
nanometers in size. This means that if one finger was the size
of the earth, it could feel the difference between a house and a
car.

* * *

Did you know that the the brain hides superfluous
information, like the second the in this sentence?

* * *

To protest against mechanization during the Industrial
Revolution, workers threw their wooden shoes - called sabots
- into the machines. This is how the word sabotage was born.

* * *

Sharks and rays are the only animals that cannot develop
cancer.

* * *

Spending more than 15,000 dollars for a wedding increases
the rate of divorce compared to couples who have a cheaper
wedding.

* * *

George Washington was known to convince voters with the help of alcohol. At an election campaign with over 400 people, he brought over 500 liters of alcohol to secure their votes.

* * *

All the branches of a tree at every stage of its height when put together are equal in thickness to the trunk

* * *

In remembrance of the deceased actor Paul Walker, Vin Diesel named his daughter Pauline.

* * *

In India, 45 percent of all residents have a mobile phone, but only 30 percent have access to a toilet.

* * *

Termites eat their food at double the speed when heavy metal is played.

* * *

Although Clint Eastwood smokes in almost all of his movies, he himself is not a smoker.

* * *

The Vatican has its own telephone company, its own radio station, its own TV station, its own stamps, its own money and its own army.

* * *

In Iceland, two-thirds of all university graduates are female.

* * *

The dress that Princess Diana wore on her wedding with Prince Charles had an 26 feet long train.

* * *

The website godtube.com describes itself as YouTube for Christians.

* * *

Pigs cannot see to the sky.

* * *

There are about nine million people in a prison around the world. 25 percent of them come from the USA.

* * *

Depending on the cause of crying, tears have a different chemical composition.

* * *

In 1980 a hospital in Las Vegas had to dismiss several employees as they were betting on when patients would die.

* * *

In China there is an app where you can order a gangster, who can take care of your enemies.

* * *

All scenes of the children of Ted Mosby in How I Met Your Mother were shot during the first season.

* * *

The modern look of the U.S. flag was designed by a school child from Ohio as a school project. His teacher gave him a B-.

* * *

Months beginning with a Sunday always have a Friday 13th.

* * *

The silk of the spider species Caeristris darwini is the toughest biomaterial in the world - ten times stronger than a comparable strand of Kevlar.

* * *

Henry Ford was the first tycoon to not let his employees work on Saturdays and Sundays, so that they could spend more time with their cars. Thus the weekend was born.

* * *

In 1906, the physicist J. J. Thompson won the Nobel Prize for his proof that electrons are particles. 31 years later his son also received the Nobel Prize for his proof that electrons are a wave.

* * *

In Ireland for a long time it was tradition that one liter of Guinness beer was given for each liter of donated blood.

* * *

Most books stolen in German universities are legal books. The second most commonly stolen books are books with a theological background.

* * *

Lake Karachay in Russia has been overrun with so much nuclear waste after World War II, that one hour of exposure is a lethal dose of radiation.

* * *

You can't commit suicide by holding your breath.

* * *

In 2012 a British man named Wesley Carrington bought a metal detector and within 20 minutes found gold from the Roman Age worth 100,000 pounds.

* * *

The Medical Students Disease describes the phenomenon of medical students suffering from the disease they recently have learned about in class.

* * *

The sign on the entrance of the town Kurt Cobain was born in, reads Come as you are.

* * *

From January 1st to December 31st of 1881, three different men - Rutherford B. Hayes, James A. Garfield and Chester A. Arthur - held the office of President of the United States.

* * *

People who laugh more frequently, live a longer life.

* * *

Ötzi suffered from lactose intolerance.

* * *

Walter Summerford was struck by lightning in his life three times. After he died, his gravestone was also struck by lightning.

* * *

On the occasion of the new Star Wars Movie The Force Awakens the weirdest products were sold under the Star Wars trade mark. Including a knife block, oranges, mascara and special Yoda water.

* * *

When the Egyptians built the pyramids, there were still mammoths roaming the earth.

* * *

A normal person can distinguish up to one million colors. Approximately three percent of the female population can, however, perceive over 100 million different colors due to an additional photoreceptor in the eye.

* * *

Before English became the dominant language in the U.S., German was the second most common language.

* * *

The letters J and Q do not occur in the periodic table of elements.

* * *

The role of the character Captain Jack Sparrow from Pirates of the Caribbean was originally given to Jim Carry. He refused as he rather wanted to make Bruce Almighty.

* * *

All people begin their lives as females. The male Y chromosome becomes active just after the fifth week of gestation.

* * *

In 1995, Newsweek published an article in which it expressed the opinion that the Internet would never make it. Meanwhile, this article is available on their website.

* * *

Researchers believe that only ten percent of our seas are explored. This means we know less about our oceans than about the moon.

* * *

The average age of soldiers fighting in Vietnam was 19. During World War II it was 26.

* * *

The Greenland shark, among others, eats polar bears and deer.

* * *

Thanks to a language computer, Stephen Hawking can speak
at a rate of one word per minute.

* * *

In Pittsburgh there is a restaurant called Conflict Kitchen. It
only serves dishes from countries the USA is in conflict with.
When the restaurant started to serve dishes from Palestine the
owners received death threats.

* * *

While tomatoes are typically classified as vegetables, they
actually belong to the fruit category.

* * *

Most board games are sold in Germany.

* * *

The slogan of Vermin Supreme, a candidate for the U.S.
presidency, was Free ponies for all Americans.

* * *

In 2008, a female shark gave birth to a pup without having
been previously fertilized. So far there are only two cases of
asexual reproduction of sharks worldwide.

* * *

Eminem repeated the ninth grade - three times.

* * *

With one pencil, one is able to draw a line with a length of up
to 37 miles.

* * *

Bob Dylans real name is Robert Allen Zimmermann

* * *

McDonald's is not the largest restaurant chain in the world.
Subway is.

* * *

Before James Bond actor Daniel Craig became a professional
actor, he could not afford to pay his rent. Because of this he
often slept on park benches.

* * *

While the mortality rate for cancer ten years ago was 215
deaths per 100,000 people, it has subsequently decreased to
172.

* * *

According to a study, men from Congo have the largest
penises.

* * *

The younger you look for your age, the higher the likelihood
to live for a long time.

* * *

Although woman are permitted to become pilots in Saudi
Arabia it is prohibited for them to drive a car.

* * *

The actor Nicolas Cage has already purchased his own grave. It is a pyramid several meters high in New Orleans.

* * *

In India, forest workers wear masks with a picture of a human face on their back of the heads so that they are not attacked by tigers.

* * *

In Newfoundland (Canada) there is a city called Dildo.

* * *

Male ants have no fathers because unfertilized ant eggs always produce male ants and only fertilized eggs produce female ants.

* * *

For blind people, who are allergic to dog hair, there are blind horses. A special breed, who are extremely small and very tame.

* * *

The first Game Boy had as much computing power needed for the first moon landing.

* * *

To investigate in a strip club in Seattle, an undercover agent visited the club 160 times and spent 16,835 dollars of tax payer money for at least 130 lap dances. Currently not one single person has been charged in this case.

* * *

Schwuugle describes itself as the gay search engine.

* * *

Beards have a health-benefit effect. They prevent pollen from entering the mouth so that the possibility of getting hay fever is decreased.

* * *

The cactus Saguaro can grow up to 20 feet tall and live for over 300 years.

* * *

The embryos of the Sandtiger shark fight each other in the mother's womb. The surviving embryo will ultimately be born.

* * *

Although Beethoven has a song called Fuer Elise, historians have proven that he did not know an Elise.

* * *

James Fixx, the creator of the word jogging died from a heart attack while jogging.

* * *

In the British Army only soldiers ranked Pioneer Sergeant are allowed to have a beard.

* * *

Approximately eight percent of human DNA is from the DNA of viruses that infected humans thousands of years ago.

* * *

Adrian Carton de Wiart fought in both World Wars and he was shot in his head, his leg, his hips and his ear. He also survived a plane crash and when the doctors were unwilling to amputate two of his fingers, he bit them off. When he was later asked about his time during the war he replied I had enjoyed the war.

* * *

Canada has more lakes than any other country in the world.

* * *

The second name of Richard Nixon was Milhouse.

* * *

Traffic in central London moves at just 10 miles per hour which is the same speed as a horse runs.

* * *

In Finland every traffic ticket is based on your personal income. The highest fine ever paid for speeding was 100,000 Euros.

* * *

About 90 percent of people won't find the the mistake in here: A,B,C,D,E,F,G,H,I,J,K,L,M,N,O,P,Q,R,S,T,U,V,W,X,Y,Z.

* * *

Based on current extrapolations Bill Gates could be the first trillionaire in the world.

* * *

A study came to the conclusion that women are more attractive to men when they do not use make-up.

* * *

After the first drive-in was opened at McDonald's in China, the system was so strange to the Chinese people that many people ordered their food from their car, parked their vehicle and then went to the restaurant to eat.

* * *

Nintendo means temple of heavenly responsibility.

* * *

On average, children start lying at the age of four.

* * *

The storming of the Bastille was mainly symbolic, at the time there were only nine prisoners who were subsequently freed.

* * *

If one donates a part of one's liver, the missing part will grow again.

* * *

Miguel Indurain, five times Tour de France winner, has a resting heart rate of 28 beats per minute.

* * *

Ioannis Economou, the chief translator of the European Parliament, speaks 32 languages fluently.

* * *

George Lucas obtained the rights to the word droid. When
Motorola released a cell phone with this name, they had to pay
a fee to George Lucas.

* * *

Dubai has an indoor ski center.

* * *

If you trace your family tree back 25 generations, you will
have 33,554,432 direct ancestors. Assuming no incest was
involved.

* * *

Based on statistics, the best drivers have the zodiac sign Leo
while the worst drivers are Taurus.

* * *

People with red hair are more resistant to anesthetics.

* * *

Most serial killers are born in November.

* * *

A 20 second hug increases the oxytocin level of people so
much that afterwards there is a much greater trust between
them.

* * *

There is no law in Denmark which prohibits breaking out of
jail.

* * *

After being hit by an avalanche, the arctic scientist Peter Freuchen freed himself by making a chisel from his frozen stool. After this, he amputated his frostbitten toes with a hammer.

* * *

The Make-A-Wish-Foundation collects money to fulfil the dreams of seriously ill children.

* * *

From 1912 to 1948 architecture was an Olympic discipline.

* * *

Originally, Mickey Mouse was called Mortimer Mouse.

* * *

In the last 150 years, the average body size of a human has increased by four inches.

* * *

A study showed that the sight of meat has a soothing effect on men.

* * *

It is impossible to pinch your nose and say Mhhh for more than three seconds.

* * *

A study from 2003 came to the conclusion that French people, among all nations, have most frequent sex.

* * *

Monhar Aich won Mr. Universe in 1952. Today he is more than 100 years old and exercises regularly at the gym.

* * *

At a height of almost 12 miles and above the air pressure is so low, that water in your body would vaporize due your own body temperature.

* * *

The most frequently visited tourist attraction in Paris is not the Eiffel Tower or the Louvre, but Disneyland.

* * *

The Swedish word for stepmother is Bonusmamma.

* * *

In 1990, the Michigan police organized a wedding of two of their undercover agents. Numerous drug dealers have been invited and were arrested during the wedding ceremony.

* * *

In 200 million years, a day on Earth will last 25 hours.

* * *

If Coca Cola was served without colorants, it would be green and not black.

* * *

Babies can already get an erection in the womb.

* * *

It is impossible to cause your own death by strangling
yourself.

* * *

An octopus has its brain in its tentacles. Even if the tentacles
are separated from the body, they continue to search for food
for a short time and bring them to a mouth which is no longer
present.

* * *

In 1972 the first black superhero to get his own comic book
series, Luke Cage was released.

* * *

In the history of the United States there have been 17
Americans who ran a marathon in less than two hours and ten
minutes. In October 2011 this was achieved by 32 Kenyans.

* * *

A short nap after studying helps the brain to remember the
materials studied better.

* * *

A nap of six minutes at midday improves memory capacity
significantly.

* * *

The two oldest cats in the world reached an age of 34 and 38.
Both belonged to the same owner. She exclusively fed her cats
bacon, eggs, broccoli and coffee.

* * *

The longest prison sentence a man ever received was 384,912 years. The sentence was received by a 22 year old postman, who had not delivered over 42,000 letters.

* * *

A study proved that 70 percent of women prefer to eat chocolate rather than have sex.

* * *

Nothing is an uninhabited town in the U.S. state of Arizona. There is nothing but a gas station and a garage.

* * *

In 1954 Bob Hawke, the future prime minister of Australia, set the world record by drinking 2.5 liters of beer in 11 seconds.

* * *